Our West

BUFFALO BILL HISTORICAL CENTER
CODY, WYOMING

OUR MISSION

The Buffalo Bill Historical Center is a museum that educates the public by advancing knowledge about the American West through acquiring, exhibiting, and interpreting collections.

TABLE OF CONTENTS

BUFFALO BILL HISTORICAL CENTER

CHARTERED 1917

The vast American West — its unmatched beauty and broad horizons—was home to diverse wildlife populations, Native American peoples, and eventually an equally diverse group of explorers, pioneers, and settlers. The wildlife and human cultures, sometimes in harmony, sometimes in conflict, made an indelible mark upon the West and its history.

Much of that western spirit is embodied in a man, William Frederick Cody, whose name and dynamism are at the core of this institution. Known as Buffalo Bill, Cody brought his version of the American West to the world through his renowned Wild West show.

By the time Cody died in 1917, the West

Robert Macfie Scriver (1914–1999)
Buffalo Bill — Plainsman, 1976
bronze, cast by Modern Art Foundry
height 86.5 inches, 12.77

A favored photography spot, this sculpture of Buffalo Bill welcomes thousands of visitors to the Center each year.

in which he lived was vanishing — and needed to be remembered. At his passing the Buffalo Bill Memorial Association was chartered. A nonprofit educational organization, the Buffalo Bill Historical Center is dedicated to exploring, preserving, and promoting the American West — its people, its wildlife, its landscapes — which Cody first introduced to the world stage more than a century ago.

Much has happened since Cody left the stage, and the passage of time has broadened our perspective. The story of the West grows increasingly robust and complex. By illuminating the highly diverse natural and cultural faces of the American West, the Buffalo Bill Historical Center brings new knowledge to bear on this distinctive region.

left:
Buffalo Bill, ca. 1913

By the turn of the century Buffalo Bill had become one of the most famous men in the world, a hero and role model for millions of children. He doted on his five grandchildren and his many nieces and nephews.

Vincent Mercaldo Collection, P.71.170

above:
William F. Cody, family and friends in front of the Irma Hotel, September, 1913.

Two future trustees are pictured: Cody's grandsons Bill (in his arms) and Fred (standing in the back seat).

F.J. Hiscock, MS6.D.OS2

BUFFALO BILL MEMORIAL ASSOCIATION

In 1927 the Buffalo Bill Memorial Association opened its original museum, a log building patterned after Cody's TE Ranch house. Under the direction of the Association and with the help of its friends and benefactors, the concept of the original museum has grown and flourished to become the five museums and library of today's Buffalo Bill Historical Center.

The Buffalo Bill Museum presents the memorabilia of Buffalo Bill and his West; the Whitney Gallery of Western Art features an unsurpassed collection of American western art; the Plains Indian Museum explores the culture of Native American people of the western plains; the Cody Firearms Museum traces the development of projectile weapons; the Draper Museum of Natural History explores the wildlife and landscapes of the Greater Yellowstone region; and the McCracken Research Library advances study of the American West through its collection of manuscripts, books, and photographs.

Each exemplifies the West; together they trace patterns of life that are uniquely American.

The Buffalo Bill Museum, 1929

Original Buffalo Bill Museum Collection, P.69.1382

Gathered for the dedication ceremony of the Buffalo Bill Museum, July 4, 1927, are (*left to right*): I.H. "Larry" Larom; J.M. Schwoob; Francis G. Cody; Mary Jester Allen; U.S. Senator John B. Kendrick of Sheridan; "Pawnee Bill" Lillie; George T. Beck; Mike Russell, an old pal of Buffalo Bill from Deadwood, South Dakota; Albert B. Cotsworth, agent for the Chicago, Burlington and Quincy Railroad; Margaret Hayden, U.S. Forest Service; Horace M. Albright, superintendent, Yellowstone National Park; E. V. Robertson; Mrs. Francis Cody.

PN.228.142

Gertrude Whitney

Original Buffalo Bill Museum Collection, P.69.511

Original dedication of *Buffalo Bill — The Scout*, July 4, 1924

Mary Jester Allen Collection, P.41.503

Gertrude Vanderbilt Whitney (1875–1942)
Buffalo Bill—The Scout, 1924
bronze, cast by Roman Bronze Works
height 149 inches

In 1922, Gertrude Vanderbilt Whitney was commissioned to create a monumental bronze sculpture of William F. "Buffalo Bill" Cody. In this dynamic equestrian sculpture, she depicted Cody in his historic role as a scout, bending down to read the trail while signaling with his rifle.

Gift of the artist, 3.58

Buffalo Bill's Boyhood Home
Built in LeClaire, Iowa, 1841

The Cody family lived in this house for two years before moving to Kansas in 1854. The Chicago, Burlington and Quincy Railroad purchased Buffalo Bill's boyhood home and moved it from Iowa to Cody in 1933. In 1948, it was donated to the Buffalo Bill Memorial Association and moved to the museum grounds. In the photo at right, Mary Jester Allen warns the house movers not to bump into the museum sign.

house, Gift of Burlington Northern Railroad,
1.69.2280; photograph, *Cody Times*
Original Buffalo Bill Museum Collection, P.69.1381

Pendant Locket, 1892

In the main gallery of the original Buffalo Bill Museum, artist Robert Lindneaux tells museum visitors about his painting, *First Scalp for Custer*.

Mary Jester Allen Collection, P.41.504

Gold and diamonds encircle the monogram for "Victoria Regina." The back is of garnet and bloodstone pressed together and inscribed, "Her Majesty, Queen Victoria to Col. W.F. Cody June 25, 1892."

Museum purchase, Garlow Collection, 1.69.309

The Whitney Gallery of Western Art, ca. 1965

Jack Richard Collection, P.89.485.1

Carl Rungius (1869–1959)
Silver Tip Grizzly Bear—Rocky Mountains, Alberta, ca. 1923
oil on canvas, 60 x 75.125 inches

Gift of Jackson Hole Preserve, Inc., 16.93.4

Remington Studio Replica

The Whitney Gallery of Western Art features a reconstruction of Frederic Remington's studio, complete with objects he collected and used.

Gift of The Coe Foundation

Hermon Atkins MacNeil (1866–1947)
The Sun Vow, modeled 1889, cast 1919
bronze, cast by Roman Bronze Works, height 34.25 inches

As a young artist, MacNeil developed an interest in Indian subjects when he saw Buffalo Bill's Wild West show perform during the *World's Columbian Exposition* in Chicago. Inspired by the dignity and grace of the Indians he saw there, he sought to create sculptures following ideals from ancient and Renaissance art.

Gift of William F. Davidson and John J. Cunningham, by exchange, 4.66

Author James Michener speaks at the dedication of the Plains Indian Museum, June, 1979.

Mrs. Henry H. Coe, chairman of the board of trustees, and trustees DeWitt Dominick and Peter Kriendler, participate with representatives of Indian tribes at the opening of the Plains Indian Museum, June, 1979. Dewey Vanderhoff photo.

Moccasins, Mesquakie, ca. 1880
length 10.25 inches, width 4.875, height 2.875 inches

Innovative design and use of color by the Eastern Plains and Prairie people are shown in the checkerboard and floral beadwork of these moccasins.

Chandler-Pohrt Collection,
Gift of the Pilot Foundation, NA.202.448

Jordan Abeyta, Shoshone-Arapaho, from Fort Washakie, Wyoming, in the Men's Fancy Dance competition, Plains Indian Museum Powwow. This powwow is an annual event held at the Buffalo Bill Historical Center in the Robbie Powwow Garden.

CODY FIREARMS MUSEUM

The Winchester Arms Museum was dedicated on July 4, 1976. Dignitaries present at the dedication ceremony included (from left to right); the Reverend R.N. Buswell; Dr. Harold McCracken, former director; actor John Wayne; William E. Talley, trustee; Clifford P. Hansen, trustee; Mrs. Henry H.R. Coe, chairman; Senator Gale McGee; and trustee Curt Gowdy.

right:
Boone and Crockett Hunting Lodge, 1991

Once housed at the Bronx Zoo, the Boone and Crockett Club's National Collection of Heads and Horns showcases North American big game animals.

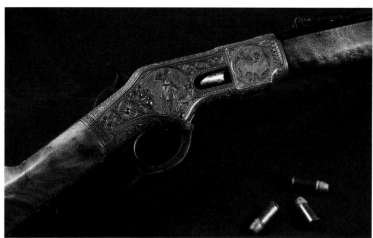

left:
Winchester Model 1866
Lever Action Deluxe Sporting Rifle, ca. 1873
Winchester Repeating Arms Co., New Haven, Conn.

Gift of the Olin Corporation, Winchester Arms Collection, 1988.8.3283

DRAPER MUSEUM OF NATURAL HISTORY

Bear 104 and her cubs were often seen and photographed in the Shoshone National Forest near the east entrance to Yellowstone National Park. She was killed by a truck in spring of 2001. The U.S. Forest Service, Wyoming Game and Fish Department, and U.S. Fish and Wildlife Service made it possible to include Bear 104 in this exhibition.

DRA.305.4

World renowned paleoanthropologist and wildlife conservationist Richard Leakey expressed his "awe" at the scope and depth of exhibits in the Draper Museum of Natural History at its dedication ceremony June 4, 2002.

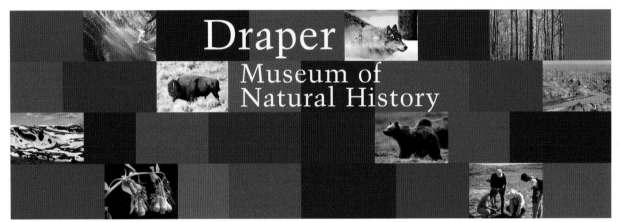

"This is a special celebration of the future of nature, and a tremendous opportunity to deal with the interrelationships of humans and wildlife species. The message is for nature, and ourselves, to be better understood and appreciated." — Richard Leakey

With roof lines echoing its dramatic Rocky Mountain backdrop, the Buffalo Bill Historical Center has evolved into one of the world's premier museums of the American West, offering distinct, but connected, interpretations of nature, history, art, and culture.

The library is named in recognition of the Buffalo Bill Historical Center's past director Dr. Harold McCracken. The collections of the McCracken Research Library are available to museum visitors and scholars of the American West.

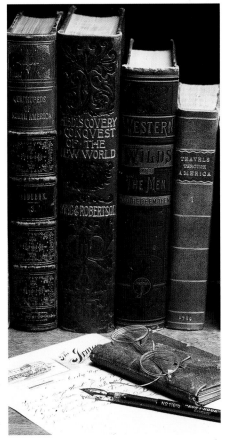

The McCracken Research Library is a specialized library and archives within the Buffalo Bill Historical Center. The collection supports research in the history and culture of the American West, with strengths in American western art and artists; the Plains Indians; Buffalo Bill Cody and the Wild West show; American firearms history and technology; and the natural history of the Greater Yellowstone region.

The Teepee Book, a magazine devoted to Indians and the Northwest, was published in Sheridan, Wyoming, in 1915 and 1916. It remains a charming example of high western culture pursued in a small western town.

AP2.T44.1915–1916

BUFFALO BILL MUSEUM

DEDICATED 1927

Within just three generations after the Civil War, the entire American West was crisscrossed with railroads and filled in with states. Settlement was rapid and disorderly. European Americans felt that they were "winning" the West and it was their destiny to tame and reclaim the wilderness and make the land economically productive.

If the experience seemed epic, no one better defined it for Americans and Europeans than Buffalo Bill Cody. And nothing turned the epic into an orderly drama better than Buffalo Bill's Wild West show.

William Frederick Cody was born in 1846 in a log cabin two miles west of the Mississippi River in Iowa Territory. His father took the family to Kansas in 1854 where young Will became part of — or witness to — the events that shaped the West. He joined a gold rush, became an expert horseman and marksman, trapped beaver, and drove a stagecoach.

During the Civil War, Cody fought for the Union with the 7th Kansas Cavalry. In 1866 he married a St. Louis woman, Louisa Frederici, who did not entirely succeed in domesticating him during their fifty-one-year marriage.

Medal of Honor

Presented by "The Congress to William F. Cody, Guide, for GALLANTRY, at Platte River, Nebr., April 26, 1872." Only four Medals of Honor were awarded to civilian scouts and guides during the Indian Wars.

1.69.2036

He earned his greatest fame as a hunter, guide, and scout for the army during the Indian Wars. Then he was persuaded to go on stage, portraying himself in "border dramas." He spent the rest of his life in show business.

Buffalo Bill started his Wild West show in Nebraska in 1883 and spent thirty years on the road, ten of them in Europe. He sank the profits from his shows in projects to help develop the modern West. Though most of them did not pay off, the legacy of his investments can be found in Arizona, Nebraska, and especially in his namesake city, Cody, Wyoming. He died in Denver in 1917 and was buried on top of Lookout Mountain overlooking the Colorado Plains.

The Buffalo Bill Museum is home to many of the personal collections of W.F. Cody and his family, as well as to a vast array of items related to his associates, his careers, and his Wild West show. The exhibition serves two purposes: to examine the personal and public lives of Buffalo Bill, and to interpret his story in the context of the history and myth of the American West.

---

left:
Irving R. Bacon (1875 – 1962)
The Life I Love (detail), 1902
oil on canvas, 22 x 34 inches

During the big game hunt commemorated in this painting, Col. William F. "Buffalo Bill" Cody chose the site for his hunting lodge, Pahaska Tepee, near the east entrance to Yellowstone National Park. Iron Tail and Black Fox, who had appeared in Cody's Wild West show, and Bishop George Allen Beecher appear in the full painting.

Bequest in memory of the
Houx and Newell Families, 15.64

Pawnee and Sioux Indians,
ca. 1886

The Pawnee and Sioux were traditional enemies on the Plains but found common ground in the Wild West show.

left to right: (Pawnee) Brave Chief, Eagle Chief, Knife Chief, Young Chief; Buffalo Bill; (Sioux) American Horse, Rocky Bear, Flies Above, Long Wolf.

Photograph by Anderson,
New York. P.69.1800

Four decades of Government issue:
Civil-War era infantryman's ammunition bag; cavalry sergeant's
fatigue jacket, 1874, and campaign hat, ca. 1875; volunteer
militia officer's dress shoulder boards, ca. 1890

In 1868 only 2,600 soldiers manned the trails, railroad routes, and
garrisons of the Great Plains. During the frontier period, the army
relied to an extraordinary extent on the loyalty, resourcefulness,
and mobility of officers and men, and on the special skills and
knowledge of civilian scouts and guides such as Buffalo Bill Cody.

bag, Gift of Olin Corporation, Winchester Arms Collection,
1988.8.3823; jacket, 1.69.1248; hat, Dr. Robert L. Anderson
Collection, 1.69.1252; shoulder boards, 1.69.1264 b/c

Buffalo-hide Coat, ca. 1870
Remington Rifle, ca. 1873

During the Indian Wars, many civilian scouts assumed flamboyant nicknames and adopted styles inspired by the dress and adornment of the Indian people among whom they lived and fought. Buffalo Bill was no exception. His buffalo-hide coat was trimmed with beaver fur and decorated with beadwork and bright tradecloth. This highly embellished rifle was presented to Cody by the Remington Company at its New York state factory in 1873.

firearm, Gift of Mr. and Mrs. Harry Schloss
in memory of Moses Kerngood, 1.69.2412; coat, 1.69.768

W.F. Cody, 1871
Green River Knife, ca. 1865

This is the earliest photograph of W.F. Cody as a young scout taken from a tintype, image reversed. He sits on the left with his Springfield rifle, "Lucretia Borgia." With Cody, left to right, are Lt. Francis Michler and Lt. Walter Scribner Schuyler. Sitting front and center is Wyndham Thomas Wyndham-Quin, Lord Adare (later the 4th Earl of Dunraven). Many scouts adapted Plains Indian styles, as this Green River knife with its brass tack decorated sheath illustrates.

photograph, P.6.906; knife, Gift of Nick Eggenhofer, 1.69.764; scabbard, Gift of Nick Eggenhofer, 1.69.765; belt, Gift of A.C. Newton, 1.69.766

Transportation in America has always suggested adventure. Travel on the frontier was a process of discovery. Means of transportation became symbols of romance—the steamboat, the clipper ship, and in the West, the stagecoach.

The stagecoach carried people in relative comfort over the rough roads of early America. The passenger compartment floated on two sets of leather springs called thoroughbraces. The motion of the coach, as Mark Twain wrote, was not unlike the rocking of a small boat.

Concord Coach, 1840

Buffalo Bill owned and used this stagecoach in his Wild West show. It is so-called because it was made by the Abbott-Downing Company of Concord, New Hampshire, painted at the factory, and shipped west.

Gift of Olive and Glenn E. Nielson, 1.69.2725

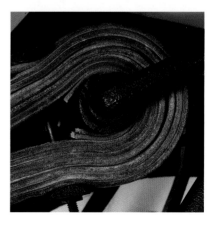

Buffalo Bill's Wild West
Stock Certificate No. 1, 1887

Buffalo Bill's Wild West began as a partnership and was incorporated before going to England for the first time. Certificate number one was issued to Cody and number two to his business partner, Nate Salsbury.

Gift of DeForest and Duer, MS6.5.OS1

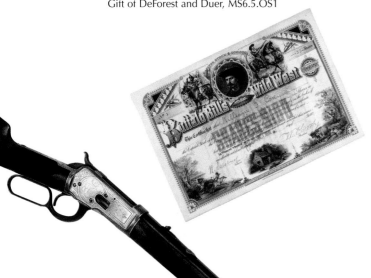

Buffalo Bill's Wild West, 1890

Hand-colored photograph by Paolo Salviati of Buffalo Bill and Indian members of the Wild West show in Venice. P.69.822

Glass Target Balls, ca. 1890

Sharpshooters in Buffalo Bill's Wild West used clay rather than glass target balls because broken glass in the arena presented a hazard. Outside the Wild West show, exhibition shooters preferred the glass balls, so organizers arranged contests in locations where the broken glass fell harmlessly into a body of water, such as a pond.

blue, 1.69.80; blue cross hatch,
Gift of Alex Kerr, 1.69.2083; amber, 1.69.1852

Winchester Rifle, Model 1892
.32 caliber, overall length 40 inches

Though she was never a shareholder, Annie Oakley, "Little Sure Shot," was one of the show's greatest assets between 1884 and 1901. This gold-plated rifle was made for Annie Oakley in 1896.

Gift of Spencer T. and Anne Olin,
1.69.1866

Dime Novels

It has been estimated that by 1900 over one billion words had been published about Buffalo Bill, mostly in dime novels like these.

top down: MS6.10.O.1.27; MS6.10.P.2.78; MS6.10.C.4.36

Buffalo Bill's Gear

The saddle is shown with a buffalo hide serape, a braided leather bridle with a six-shooter bit made for Buffalo Bill by a prisoner in Colorado State Penitentiary, and beaded buckskin gauntlets.

saddle, ca. 1895, made by Collins and Morrison of Omaha, William Cody Boal Collection, 1.69.45; bridle and bit, ca. 1915, Mary Jester Allen Collection, 1.69.44 a/b; gauntlets, ca. 1885, Gift of Mrs. S.W. Harding, 1.69.2661

left:
The Rough Riders of the World in a Grand Ethnological Congress lithograph poster, 1910

This poster advertising Buffalo Bill's Wild West was made by U.S. Lithograph Co., Russell-Morgan Print, Cincinnati.

1.69.112

THE WYOMING DISPATCH.

VOLUME 1.

A Fearless Newspaper, Devoted to the Interests of the Great Big Horn Basin.

CODY, BIG HORN COUNTY, WYOMING, JULY 18, 1902.

Published at the Gateway to the National Park.

NUMBER 26.

MONSTER SHOE SALE

Bigger Bargains Than Ever.

Our July shoe clearance is bound to be a success because we have cut the price way down. We have placed on sale a large assortment of men's, women's, misses, boy's and children's shoes, and marked them far below our "cut-the-prices-in-two" sale and you know what that means. Let us quote you a few prices.

MEN'S SHOES...

MISSES' SHOES $1

Children's Shoes 75c

Cut In Men's Shoes.

Oxford Shoe Sale.

20% Discount On Kirkendall Shoes.

Biggest Shoe Sale Yet.

H. P. ARNOLD & Co.

THE BIG STORE

Cody Trading Company

Cody, Wyoming

The Wyoming Dispatch, July 18, 1902

As this issue went to press in Cody, Buffalo Bill was performing with his Wild West show in Hancock, Michigan. The checks show, however, that his mind was never far from his interests in the West. In the town of Cody alone, his investments in 1902 would total more than $100,000.

dispatch, Gift of Mrs. Agnes B. Chamberlain, MS5.9.MC.7; checks from Nebraska, Colorado, and Arizona Banks, MS6.1.C.1.20

Babcock Drum-Cylinder Printing Press, ca. 1895

The most important ingredient for success for any new town on the frontier, other than a post office, was a newspaper. This printing press was purchased by W.F. Cody for the *Cody Enterprise* in 1899.

Gift of Mr. and Mrs. George Abrahamson, 1.69.1843

William F. Cody (detail), 1912

William F. Cody relaxing during a business trip to Tampa, Florida.

P.6.290

Edison Cylinder Phonograph and Cylinders, ca. 1900

W.F. Cody and his family, like most Americans, were excited by the technological progress represented by Thomas Edison's inventions. Cody and Edison were equally celebrated by the French at the *Centennial Exposition* in Paris in 1889, where Cody and Edison became friends and mutual admirers.

cabinet, Gift of the Quintin Blair Family, 1.69.5366; cylinders, Buffalo Bill Buffs Fund, 1.69.5355

Arta Cody Boal's Silk Moire Wedding Dress, 1889
Letter to Buffalo Bill from daughter Arta, 1889

W.F. Cody was in Europe with his Wild West show when his daughter Arta married Horton Boal at the family home in North Platte, Nebraska; this is the letter she wrote on the eve of her wedding. Only two of Cody's four children survived to adulthood—Arta, the eldest, and Irma Cody Garlow, the youngest.

dress, Gift of Mr. and Mrs. Robert L. Hayden, 1.69.2041; letter, MS6.1.B.3.5

WHITNEY GALLERY OF WESTERN ART

DEDICATED 1959

The Whitney Gallery of Western Art presents the creative accomplishments of artists who explored, documented, celebrated, and interpreted the American West. One of the most important collections of American western art, the Whitney gives a comprehensive overview of the development of western art from the early nineteenth century to the present day. The works embrace the range of styles encountered in American art, including realism, romanticism, impressionism, and expressionism.

The subject of the American West — its land, people, and wildlife — is the linking thread. In the Whitney Gallery, the West can be seen as a specific place embodied in scenes of the Rocky Mountains, Indian encampments, cattle ranches, and other locations in the region. The West is also an idea, or even a myth, interpreted in visions of an American Eden, an untamed wilderness, and a land of opportunity, courage, and cultural values.

Frederic Remington (1861–1909)
Radisson and Groseilliers, 1905
oil on canvas, 17.125 x 30.125 inches

Remington became one of the most famous western artists through his archetypal depictions of the Wild West — bucking broncos, danger, and conflict. Late in his career, as he loosened his brushstrokes and experimented with color, he painted masterworks such as *Radisson and Groseilliers,* which portray a more harmonious encounter with the frontier.

Gift of Mrs. Karl Frank, 14.86

The Whitney collection includes paintings by such early explorer artists as George Catlin, Alfred Jacob Miller, and John Mix Stanley. The glories of the western lands are revealed in landscapes by Albert Bierstadt and Thomas Moran. Frederic Remington and Charles M. Russell lead the artists who depicted the Wild West of the late nineteenth century and influenced early twentieth century illustrators such as N.C. Wyeth and W.H.D. Koerner. Finally, the Whitney Gallery exhibits paintings and sculptures by contemporary artists, such as James Bama, Fritz Scholder, and Harry Jackson, whose works represent viewpoints on the modern West.

The masterworks on view at the Whitney celebrate the artistic impulse enriched by the American encounter with the West. These paintings, sculptures, and prints are not only beautiful and striking in their own right, they have shaped our concepts of the meaning of the West.

Paul Manship (1885–1966)
Indian and Pronghorn Antelope, 1914
bronze: Indian, height 13.5 inches;
antelope, height 12.5 inches
far left: (detail)

Manship united classical concern for precisely modeled forms with a modern streamlined sensibility, creating a style that was a forerunner of Art Deco. Interested in mythology, he portrayed the American Indian not with physical realism, but as a symbolic figure, evoking the power of the hunt.

Gift of the William E. Weiss Fund and
Mr. and Mrs. Richard J. Schwartz, 3.89 a/b

William Ranney (1813–1857)
Advice on the Prairie, 1853
oil on canvas, 38.75 x 55.25 inches

Ranney painted genre paintings — scenes of everyday life. In this work he portrayed a group of western immigrants, including a family, camped with their wagon for the evening. A mountain man, the representative of an earlier period of frontier history, tells them a tale of what they will encounter.

Gift of Mrs. J. Maxwell Moran, 10.91

George Catlin (1796–1872)
Rain-Making, Mandan, ca. 1855–1870
oil on paperboard, 18.125 x 24.625 inches

Believing that Indians soon would vanish, Catlin traveled west with the mission of recording tribal customs and appearances to preserve them. He saw the Indian as a primitive man, living in unity with nature. Self-taught, Catlin developed a simplified style with strong lines and bold contrasts of color.

Gift of Paul Mellon, 24.86

John Mix Stanley (1814–1872)
Last of Their Race, 1857
oil on canvas, 43 x 60 inches

An allegory on the theme of the Indian as a dying race, this painting depicts remnants of tribes pushed to the edge of the ocean with the sun in the distance and buffalo skulls forecasting the end. Stanley arranged the figures in a pyramid, giving a classical composition to the painting.

5.75

right:
Albert Bierstadt (1830–1902)
Yellowstone Falls, ca. 1881
oil on canvas, 44.25 x 30.5 inches

Bierstadt painted this view of the Lower Falls after his 1881 trip to Yellowstone National Park. He loaned this painting to the White House and tried to convince Congress to purchase it for the President's residence, but was never successful. It helped, however, to inspire President Chester A. Arthur to visit Yellowstone in 1883.

Gift of Mr. and Mrs. Lloyd Taggart, 2.63

Rosa Bonheur (1822–1899)
Col. William F. Cody, 1889
oil on canvas, 18.5 x 15.25 inches

Buffalo Bill enthralled Europeans with his Wild West show when he took it to Paris in 1889. He accepted the invitation of Rosa Bonheur to visit her chateau in Fontainebleau, where she probably painted this portrait. She in turn visited the grounds of Buffalo Bill's Wild West to sketch the exotic American animals.

Given in Memory of William R. Coe
and Mai Rogers Coe, 8.66

Thomas Moran (1837–1926)
Golden Gate, Yellowstone National Park, 1893
oil on canvas, 36.25 x 50.25 inches

Moran's name became synonymous with Yellowstone. After he accompanied the official governmental expedition into the region in 1871, his sketches of the wonders helped to convince Congress to establish Yellowstone as the first national park. The artist returned to the park in 1892 and painted this view of the Golden Gate pass.

4.75

top right:
Henry Farny (1847–1916)
Days of Long Ago, 1903
oil on paper mounted on board,
37.5 x 23.75 inches

Farny traveled west as a magazine illustrator at the end of the nineteenth century and was familiar with changes affecting Native American life after the Indian Wars. In easel paintings, such as *Days of Long Ago*, he created nostalgic visions of a bygone past.

6.75

right:
N.C. Wyeth (1882–1945)
The Lee of the Grub-Wagon,
1904–1905
oil on canvas, 38 x 26 inches

In 1904 Wyeth made his first trip to the West. He worked for three weeks on a Colorado cattle roundup which provided the inspiration for a series of paintings about cowboys.

Gift of John M. Schiff, 46.83

Charles M. Russell (1864–1926)
When Law Dulls the Edge of Chance, 1915
oil on canvas, 30 x 48 inches

Known as the "cowboy artist," Russell is often appreciated for his insider's view of western life. His own experiences as a wrangler influenced his paintings and sculpture, but he also used historical events and imagination in works such as this depiction of horse thieves intercepted by the Royal Canadian Mounted Police.

Gift of William E. Weiss, 28.78

Maynard Dixon (1875–1946)
The Medicine Robe, 1915
oil on canvas, 40 x 30 inches

Experimenting with an impressionistic painting style and drawing upon his experiences working in the desert light of the West, California-born Dixon created this powerful image of a Northern Plains Indian.

Gift of Mr. and Mrs. Godwin Pelissero, 2.73

Joseph Henry Sharp (1859–1953)
The Broken Bow, ca. 1912
oil on canvas, 44.5 x 59.375 inches

In the early years of the twentieth century, Sharp divided his time between painting the Northern Plains Indians of Montana and the Southwestern Indians of New Mexico. In this tender subject of family life, he combined the two groups, using Plains clothing and an adobe setting.

7.75

Frederic Remington (1861–1909)
The Rattlesnake, ca. 1905
bronze, cast by Roman Bronze Works
height 22.625 inches

Remington used the subject of the horse reacting to the rattlesnake to create one of his most daring sculptures. He modeled the horse as a dynamic curve pulling away from the small, but deadly, snake. Dissatisfied with his first version of this sculpture, Remington reworked it extensively to create this larger, more compact version.

Gift of The Coe Foundation, 50.61

W.H.D. Koerner (1878–1938)
Madonna of the Prairie, 1921
oil on canvas, 37 x 28.75 inches

In the novel *The Covered Wagon*, Molly Wingate traveled the Oregon Trail with a wagon train of settlers. Encountering prairie fires and Indian arrows, the beautiful maiden eventually reached Oregon, where, in the conventions of popular fiction, she found true love. In this illustration for the book jacket of the novel, Koerner used the covered wagon to form a halo around the pioneer's head.

25.77

James Earle Fraser (1876–1953)
End of the Trail, modeled 1894; reworked 1915; cast after 1918
bronze, cast by Roman Bronze Works, height 33.75 inches

End of the Trail has appealed to public sentiment since its conception following Chicago's 1893 *World's Columbian Exposition*. Inspired by the exposition's fusing of the nostalgic with the progressive, Fraser created a windblown and destitute symbol which represented the public's belief in the sad but inevitable extinction of the Indian.

Clara Peck Purchase Fund, 112.67

James Bama (b. 1926)
A Contemporary Sioux Indian, 1978
oil on panel, 23.375 x 35.375 inches

A Contemporary Sioux Indian is Bama's statement on the rejection of traditional Native American culture in main-stream American society. The decaying background reads NO PARKING VIOLATORS TOWED AWAY. The artist's realistic style comes from an attentive painting method that uses both photographs and sketches as preparation.

William E. Weiss Contemporary Art Fund Purchase, 19.78

Fritz Scholder (1937–2005)
Indian with Tomahawk, 1970
oil on canvas, 58.25 x 58.25 inches

In a series on Indians begun in 1967, Scholder sought new and innovative pictorial representations to convey the harsh realities of the contemporary Indian's world. He often uses bold, unnatural colors and distorted images with loose painterly brushwork to create his personal vision of the Indian's reality.

William E. Weiss Contemporary Art Fund Purchase, 15.77

PLAINS INDIAN MUSEUM

DEDICATED 1979

The experiences of the Plains Indian people include some of the most dramatic episodes in the history of the American West. The people known by the tribal names of Arapaho, Cheyenne, Kiowa, Comanche, Blackfeet, Sioux, Shoshone, and Pawnee, among others, once dominated the vast open region of the Great Plains stretching from the Mississippi River to the Rocky Mountains. Through its outstanding collection and interpretive programs, the Plains Indian Museum explores the cultural histories and artistry of these people from their buffalo hunting past to the living traditions of the present.

At the beginning of the nineteenth century, the people of the Plains lived as farmers in villages along streams and fertile river valleys, and as hunters in tipi camps in the tall grass prairies where vast herds of buffalo grazed. Their food and other necessities were taken from buffalo, deer, elk, and other game, and the wild plants of the region. From warriors' feathered war bonnets, shields, and lances to hide clothing, moccasins, and ceremonial rattles and fans, objects were beautifully decorated with natural pigments, porcupine quills, and trade beads.

By the end of the nineteenth century, Plains Indian people faced confinement on reservations, which ended their lives as buffalo hunters. The clothing and ceremonial objects of reservation life illustrate not only older traditions, but also the introduction of new ideas, materials, and designs.

The Adversity and Renewal Gallery of the Plains Indian Museum completes the story of the survival of the Plains Indian people and their most important traditions. The beadwork, powwow clothing, paintings, sculptures, and other examples of contemporary art reflect this cultural survival in a changing world.

Eagle Hat, Crow, ca. 1870
length 26 inches, height 11 inches

With its special power and beauty, the eagle is the bird most revered by Plains Indian people. This hat is composed of an eagle head, wing, and tail feathers over buffalo hide; it is trimmed with brass bells and has brass button eyes.

Gift of the I.H. "Larry" Larom Collection of
Plains Indian Ethnology, NA.203.168

left:
Grizzly Bear Claw Necklace (detail),
made by John Young Bear, Mesquakie, ca. 1920
necklace, length 18.5 inches, width 13.5 inches;
trailer, length 60 inches

Worn by men of the Eastern Plains, grizzly bear claw necklaces were highly valued because they reflected the strength and courage of the bear. This necklace is made of otter fur, beads, and forty bear claws.

Adolph Spohr Collection, Gift of Larry Sheerin,
NA.203.213

right:
Dress, Lakota, ca. 1900
length 45 inches

Since the late 1800s, Sioux women have created dresses with heavily beaded yokes in bold designs. This type of dress was worn only for special occasions.

Gift of Mr. and Mrs. William Henry Harrison,
NA.202.70

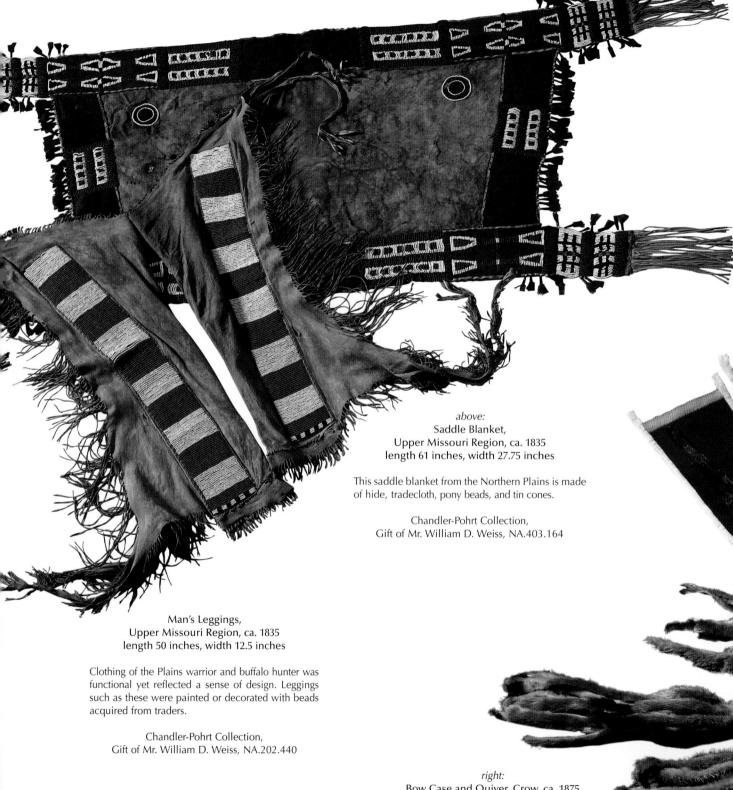

above:
Saddle Blanket,
Upper Missouri Region, ca. 1835
length 61 inches, width 27.75 inches

This saddle blanket from the Northern Plains is made
of hide, tradecloth, pony beads, and tin cones.

Chandler-Pohrt Collection,
Gift of Mr. William D. Weiss, NA.403.164

Man's Leggings,
Upper Missouri Region, ca. 1835
length 50 inches, width 12.5 inches

Clothing of the Plains warrior and buffalo hunter was
functional yet reflected a sense of design. Leggings
such as these were painted or decorated with beads
acquired from traders.

Chandler-Pohrt Collection,
Gift of Mr. William D. Weiss, NA.202.440

right:
Bow Case and Quiver, Crow, ca. 1875
strap, length 57 inches, width 6.75 inches;
case, length 31.5 inches

Hunting, whether with bows, arrows, lances, or later
with trade guns, provided food and raw materials for
clothing, tools, and shelter. This bow case and quiver
are made of otter hide, wool, and beads.

Adolph Spohr Collection, Gift of Larry Sheerin,
NA.102.20

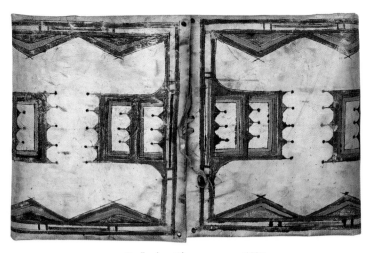

Parfleche, Cheyenne, ca. 1885
length 23.5 inches, width 14.75 inches

Parfleches, made of folded rawhide, were used to carry clothing, food, and other belongings when Plains Indian people traveled. Painted in geometric designs, parfleches often were made in pairs to be tied to each side of a horse.

Chandler-Pohrt Collection,
Gift of Mr. William D. Weiss, NA.106.147

Shields were made of thick pieces of rawhide and painted with symbols created to provide strength to the warrior. Animal figures were frequently used on both shields and their covers.

Shield Cover, Crow, ca. 1870
diameter 19.25 inches

This shield cover is made of buckskin, buffalo hide, and ermine.

Adolph Spohr Collection, Gift of Larry Sheerin, NA.108.16

Shield Cover, Crow, ca.1860
diameter 21.5 inches

A painted bear and his tracks, a charm, and a flicker feather make up the design of this buckskin shield cover.

Chandler-Pohrt Collection,
Gift of Mr. and Mrs. Edson W. Spencer, NA.108.105

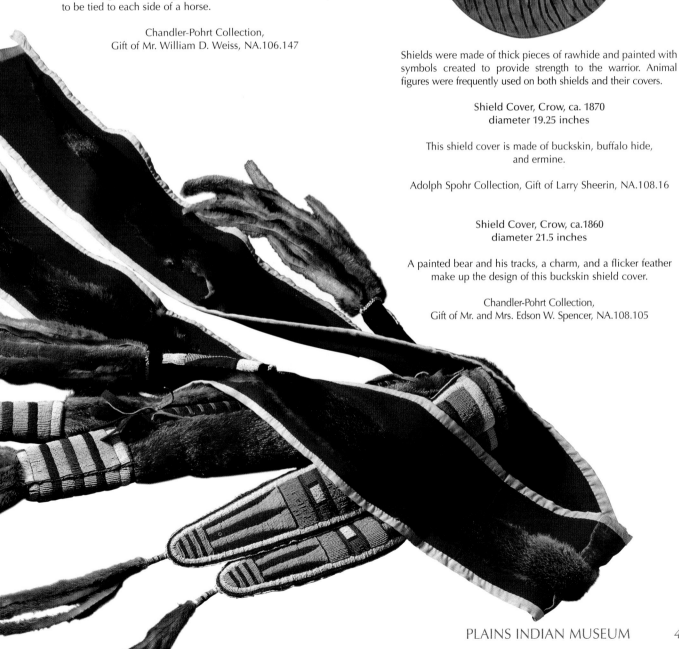

left:
Ghost Dance Dress,
Southern Arapaho, ca. 1890
length 54 inches

The Arapaho were instrumental in spreading the doctrines of the Ghost Dance to other tribes. The design of this Arapaho dress depicts stars represented by crosses and a crescent moon.

Chandler-Pohrt Collection,
Gift of Mary J. and James R. Jundt, NA.204.4

right:
Ghost Dance Dress,
Southern Arapaho, ca. 1890
length 56 inches

Hide dresses, shirts, and leggings with painted symbols of the sky, such as the stars and moon, were made for the Ghost Dance.

Gift of J.C. "Kid" Nichols, NA.204.1

In 1890 Plains Indian people faced poverty, disease, and death on reservations. Under the leadership of the Paiute visionary Wovoka, the Ghost Dance religion revived the hopes of many of the tribes. Wovoka taught that the people could bring about the renewal of the world by working hard, living peacefully, and doing the Ghost Dance. The buffalo and other game would be plentiful, dead relatives and friends would return, and white men would disappear.

Ghost Dance Shirt, Arapaho, ca. 1890
length 40 inches

Designs for Ghost Dance clothing often came to individuals in visions that occurred during the ceremonies. The turtle, seen on this shirt, was symbolic to the Arapaho of the spirit world. Eagles, crows, and magpies were considered messengers to the heavens.

Chandler-Pohrt Collection,
Gift of Searle Family Trust and
The Paul Stock Foundation, NA.204.5

Salish Cradle, 1919
length 34.5 inches, width 15 inches

Cradles continued to be made and used after Plains Indian people left the buffalo hunting way of life. This beaded Salish cradle with floral designs could have been made for a special occasion.

Simplot Collection,
Gift of J.R. Simplot, NA.111.57

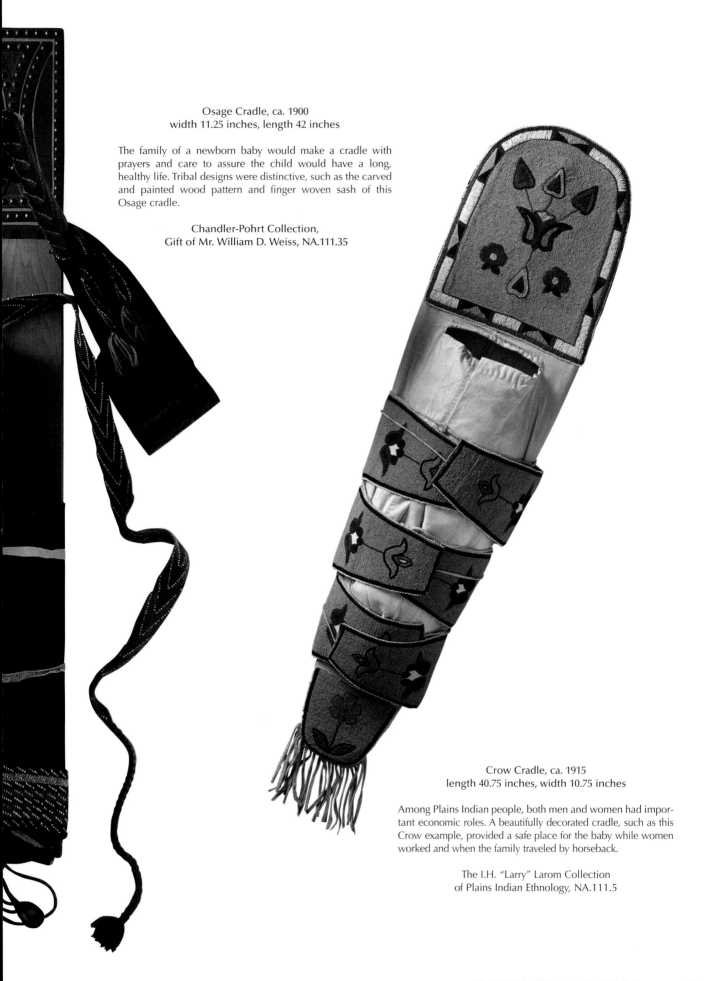

Osage Cradle, ca. 1900
width 11.25 inches, length 42 inches

The family of a newborn baby would make a cradle with prayers and care to assure the child would have a long, healthy life. Tribal designs were distinctive, such as the carved and painted wood pattern and finger woven sash of this Osage cradle.

Chandler-Pohrt Collection,
Gift of Mr. William D. Weiss, NA.111.35

Crow Cradle, ca. 1915
length 40.75 inches, width 10.75 inches

Among Plains Indian people, both men and women had important economic roles. A beautifully decorated cradle, such as this Crow example, provided a safe place for the baby while women worked and when the family traveled by horseback.

The I.H. "Larry" Larom Collection
of Plains Indian Ethnology, NA.111.5

The Native American Church combines elements of traditional tribal religions and Christianity. Developed during the 1890s, this religious movement continues to be an important force in the lives of many Plains Indian people.

Native American Church Box, Fan,
Gourd Rattle, and Pin, Northern Cheyenne, ca. 1950

box, height 9.5 inches, length 19.25 inches, width 5.5 inches;
fan, length 15 inches; pin, length 2 inches, width 2.5 inches;
gourd rattle, length 23 inches

Decorated boxes, such as this one with a hand carved and painted design, are used to carry fans, rattles, staffs, and other objects used in Native American Church meetings.

Anne Black Collection, NA.502.47.1–6

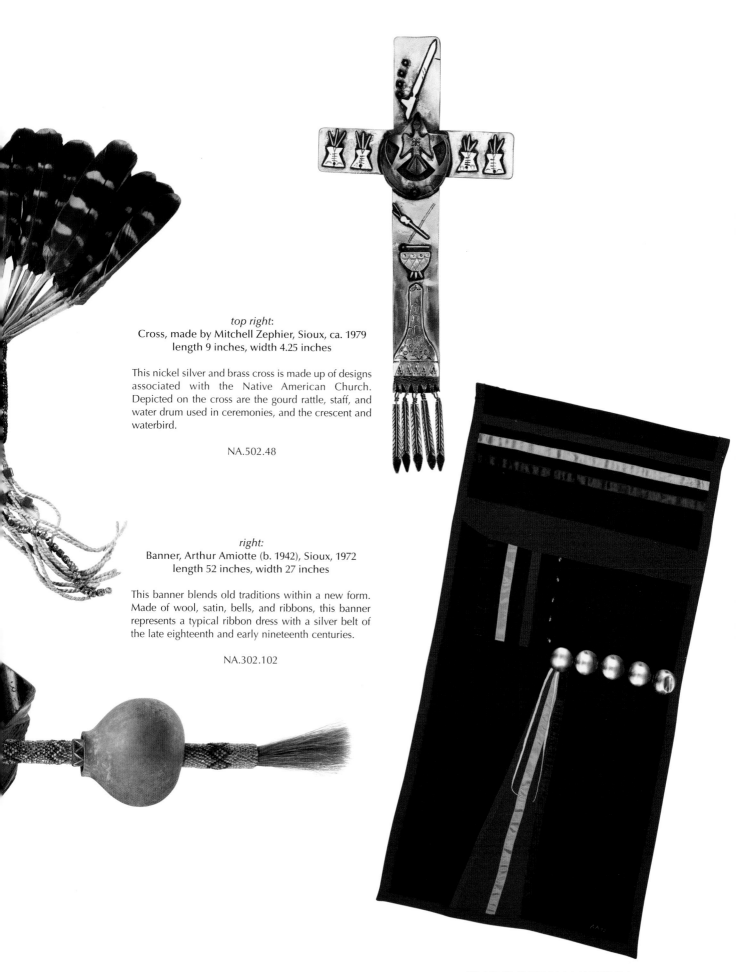

top right:
Cross, made by Mitchell Zephier, Sioux, ca. 1979
length 9 inches, width 4.25 inches

This nickel silver and brass cross is made up of designs associated with the Native American Church. Depicted on the cross are the gourd rattle, staff, and water drum used in ceremonies, and the crescent and waterbird.

NA.502.48

right:
Banner, Arthur Amiotte (b. 1942), Sioux, 1972
length 52 inches, width 27 inches

This banner blends old traditions within a new form. Made of wool, satin, bells, and ribbons, this banner represents a typical ribbon dress with a silver belt of the late eighteenth and early nineteenth centuries.

NA.302.102

CODY FIREARMS MUSEUM

DEDICATED 1991

The Cody Firearms Museum houses the most comprehensive and important collection of American firearms in the world. It chronicles the development of American and European firearms from the sixteenth century to the present. Replicas of a colonial gun shop and a frontier stage stop document the influence of firearms on the settlement of the United States. A late nineteenth century factory and a western hardware store exhibit the fundamental contributions of the firearms industry to the industrial revolution.

At the heart of the Cody Firearms Museum is the Winchester Arms Collection. Previously housed at the Winchester factory in New Haven, Connecticut, the collection came to the Buffalo Bill Historical Center in 1975 as a loan from the Olin Corporation. During the period of 1976–1981, the Winchester Collection was on view within the Buffalo Bill Museum.

German Flintlock Pocket Pistol, ca. 1710
.33 caliber
overall length 5.875 inches, barrel length 2.5 inches

Even before the introduction of the well-known Deringer pistol of the nineteenth century, small pistols, such as this one made by L.Weber of Berlin, were popular personal sidearms.

Gift of Olin Corporation, Winchester Arms Collection
1988.8.229

Beginning in 1981, it was displayed separately as the Winchester Arms Museum in a specially designed gallery on the lower level. The Olin Corporation formally gave the collection to the Center in 1988. Construction of a new wing was completed in the spring of 1991, and the Cody Firearms Museum opened to the public on June 22, 1991.

In addition to its encyclopedic firearms collection, which represents the work of most major American arms makers, the Cody Firearms Museum has an important research collection of nineteenth and early twentieth century engineering and design drawings, production records, and advertising materials.

The Cody Firearms Museum is also the current home of the Boone and Crockett Club's National Collection of Heads and Horns, one of the finest assemblages of big game mounts in the world.

left:
Winchester Model 1895 Sporting Rifle,
engraver, Philip Clundt
serial number 403014, 1917
.30-06 caliber
overall length 42 inches,
barrel length 24 inches

This highly decorated sporting rifle was presented to novelist Zane Gray by Winchester Repeating Arms Company.

Donated in Loving Memory of Robert Jesse Moore by his family, 1991.1.1

right:
Engineering Design Drawings and Browning Bros. Prototype Model 1893 Shotgun

Design drawings are critical elements in the development of firearms. These drawings help to document the design process that accompanied the creation of the Model 1893 shotgun as well as other models.

Gift of Olin Corporation, Winchester Arms Collection, firearm, 1988.8.1193; drawings, MS20

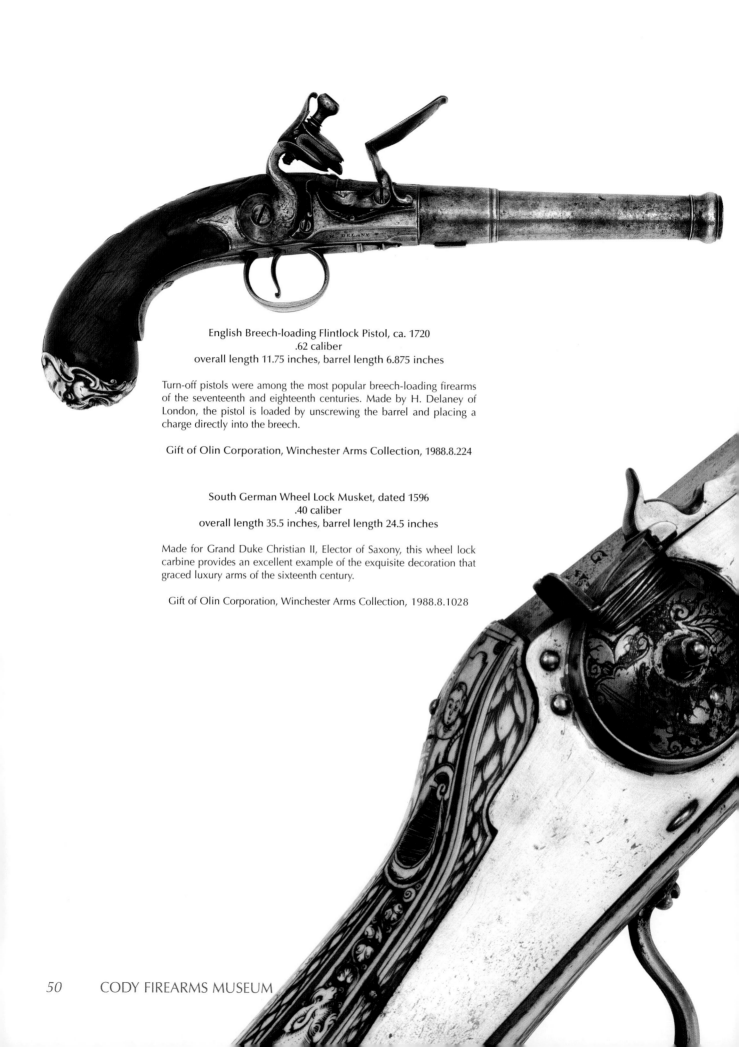

English Breech-loading Flintlock Pistol, ca. 1720
.62 caliber
overall length 11.75 inches, barrel length 6.875 inches

Turn-off pistols were among the most popular breech-loading firearms of the seventeenth and eighteenth centuries. Made by H. Delaney of London, the pistol is loaded by unscrewing the barrel and placing a charge directly into the breech.

Gift of Olin Corporation, Winchester Arms Collection, 1988.8.224

South German Wheel Lock Musket, dated 1596
.40 caliber
overall length 35.5 inches, barrel length 24.5 inches

Made for Grand Duke Christian II, Elector of Saxony, this wheel lock carbine provides an excellent example of the exquisite decoration that graced luxury arms of the sixteenth century.

Gift of Olin Corporation, Winchester Arms Collection, 1988.8.1028

**American and European Powder Horns and Flasks,
mid-nineteenth century**

This group of powder horns and flasks is representative of those commonly
used in North America and Europe between 1780 and 1850.

Gift of Olin Corporation, Winchester Arms Collection,

flasks: *top left to right*: 1988.8.3905; 1988.8.3903;
lower left to right: 1988.8.3670; 1988.8.3980;
horn, 1988.8.3666

European Flintlock Muskets, Fowlers, and Fusils, mid-eighteenth to mid-nineteenth centuries

During the Colonial period, America relied on Europe for her firearms. Most muskets used by American forces during the Revolution were imported. Even hunting guns, such as fowlers, assembled in America, were usually fitted with foreign-made barrels and flintlocks. The well-made European flintlock fusil was the Native American's choice of firearm well into the nineteenth century.

Gift of Olin Corporation, Winchester Arms Collection, *left to right:*
1988.8.569; 1988.8.596; 1988.8.592; 1988.8.593; 1988.8.1328

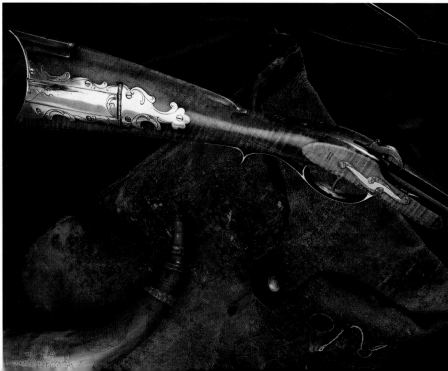

American Percussion Rifle, ca. 1815
.43 caliber
overall length 52.25 inches, barrel length 36 inches

Soon after its development in England, the percussion ignition system spread to the United States. This Pennsylvania-style rifle made by J. Coe was fitted with a pill-lock percussion ignition system rather than the traditional flintlock.

Gift of Olin Corporation, Winchester Arms Collection, firearm, 1988.8.1127; horn, 1988.8.1258

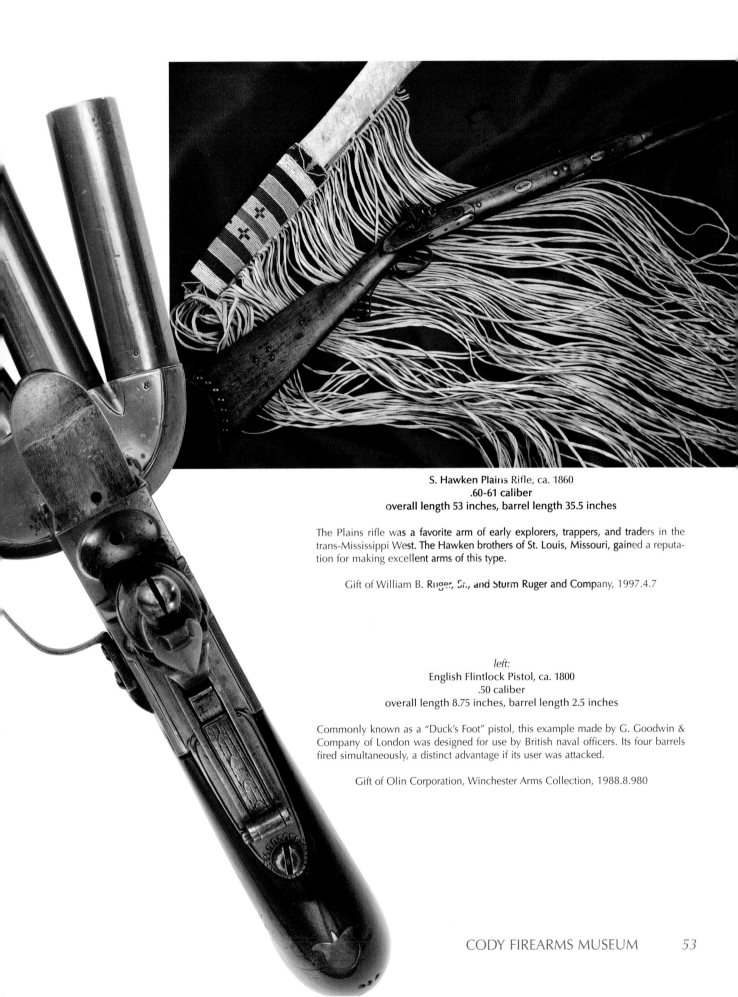

S. Hawken Plains Rifle, ca. 1860
.60-61 caliber
overall length 53 inches, barrel length 35.5 inches

The Plains rifle was a favorite arm of early explorers, trappers, and traders in the trans-Mississippi West. The Hawken brothers of St. Louis, Missouri, gained a reputation for making excellent arms of this type.

Gift of William B. Ruger, Sr., and Sturm Ruger and Company, 1997.4.7

left:
English Flintlock Pistol, ca. 1800
.50 caliber
overall length 8.75 inches, barrel length 2.5 inches

Commonly known as a "Duck's Foot" pistol, this example made by G. Goodwin & Company of London was designed for use by British naval officers. Its four barrels fired simultaneously, a distinct advantage if its user was attacked.

Gift of Olin Corporation, Winchester Arms Collection, 1988.8.980

American Percussion Pocket Pistols, ca. 1855
.47 caliber
overall length 6.25 inches, barrel length 2.5 inches

Patterned after the famous pocket pistols by Deringer, these pistols by G. Erichson of Houston, Texas, provide a graphic example of the excellent work done by gunsmiths living on the edges of the American frontier.

Gift of Olin Corporation, Winchester Arms Collection, 1988.8.237

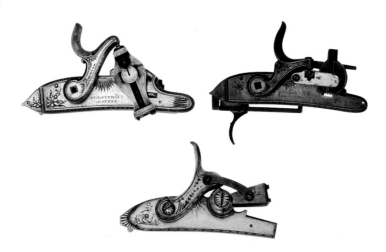

English and French Detached Percussion Pistol Locks, ca. 1805–1820

The Rev. Alexander Forsyth, a Scottish minister, was an avid sportsman and inventor. His invention of the percussion ignition system was the most important development in the evolution of firearms since the introduction of gunpowder.

top down: 1983.6.1; 1983.6.2; 1983.6.3

American Air Pistol, ca. 1869–1872
.25 caliber
overall length 10.25 inches, barrel length 5.25 inches

Widely marketed after the Civil War, low-cost air pistols, such as this one by E.H. Hawley, were intended for indoor use. Target shooting with air pistols was a popular and inexpensive form of entertainment.

Gift of Olin Corporation, Winchester Arms Collection, 1988.8.1008

right:
Colt Model 1873 Single Action Revolver, serial number 51193, 1879
.44 caliber
overall length 13 inches, barrel length 7.5 inches

Also known as the "Peacemaker" and "Frontier Six-shooter," the Colt Model 1873 is the revolver that most think of as a symbol of the Wild West.

Gift of Lillian E. Herring in memory of Major William H. Herring, 1988.9.1

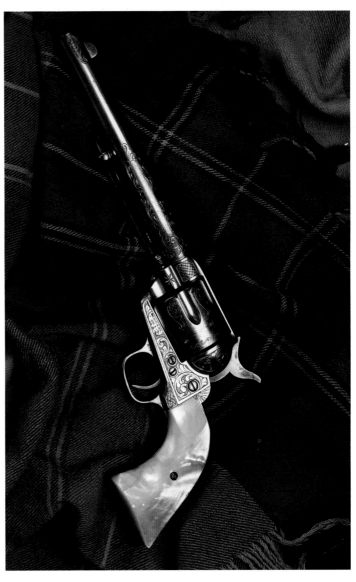

Firearms Factory Replica

During the late nineteenth century the firearms industry was responsible for many of the design innovations that made modern manufacturing methods possible. Many of the machines in use today have their origins in the firearms factories of that period.

Gift of the Savage Arms Company,
1991.19.1; 1991.19.2; 1991.19.3

Winchester Model 1894 Lever Action Rifle,
serial number 154222, 1902
.30 caliber
overall length 44.5 inches, barrel length 26 inches

Several members of the renowned Ulrich family of engravers worked for the Winchester Repeating Arms Company. This deluxe takedown version of the Model 1894 was engraved and inlaid with gold by John Ulrich.

Gift of Olin Corporation, Winchester Arms Collection,
rifle, 1988.8.1243;
calendars, *left to right*: 1988.8.2911; 1988.8.2914

Colt Model 1855 Percussion Pocket Pistol,
serial number 17, 1855
.28 caliber
overall length 7.75 inches, barrel length 3.25 inches

Over the years, the name Colt has become a synonym for the revolver. This Model 1855 pocket pistol was engraved by Gustave Young, one of the foremost American engravers of the nineteenth century.

firearm, Gift of Larry Sheerin, 1988.13.1.1;
jacket, Gift of the Irving H. "Larry" Larom Estate, 1.69.2027

Cylinders for
American and European Revolvers,
nineteenth and twentieth centuries

Although firearms equipped with revolving cylinders had been made for some time, they were not produced in large numbers until the middle of the nineteenth century.

cylinders, Cody Firearms Museum Collection

DRAPER MUSEUM OF NATURAL HISTORY

DEDICATED 2002

The Draper Museum of Natural History is the newest addition to the Buffalo Bill Historical Center and the first major American natural history museum established in the twenty-first century. The Draper is a new breed of museum that joins two great lineages — the Buffalo Bill Historical Center and the world's great natural history museums of the nineteenth and twentieth centuries.

The Draper integrates science and natural history with cultural history to explore, document, and interpret the rich fabric of the Greater Yellowstone region. This region is often regarded as the last remnant of the wild American West and is one of the most compelling ecological theaters in the world. Just as Yellowstone National Park inspired the creation of other conservation strongholds across the world, events in the Greater Yellowstone region continue to carry global implications for how humans coexist with wild nature. The Draper is dedicated to illuminating the complex relationships among humans, wildlife, and landscapes with an eye toward shaping the future by understanding the past.

C.R. Preston

Golden-mantled ground squirrels live in rocky outcrops in the Greater Yellowstone region, including alpine tundra. Rock crevices provide protection from weasels, foxes, coyotes, raptors, and other predators.

The Draper's central exhibition gallery, Alpine-to-Plains Trail, winds along a descending path through Alpine, Mountain Forest, Mountain Meadow/Aquatic, and Plains/Basin environments that comprise much of the Greater Yellowstone region. In each environment, we present stories of Yellowstone's wildlife, landscape, and people, richly illustrated with natural history specimens, photographs, and audiovisual recordings, together with artwork and artifacts representing the other museums of the Buffalo Bill Historical Center.

Our immersive exhibitions are only a fraction of the Draper experience. We extend the museum walls with field-based research and programming that take advantage of our location in one of the greatest natural laboratories on Earth. Draper staff, students, interns, and volunteers participate in hands-on fieldwork that enriches our in-house exhibitions and programs. All museums are valued for their collections — the Draper is valued for its collections, research, and interpretation in the Greater Yellowstone region.

left: An elk carcass provides a feast and battleground for scavengers. The immersive exhibition galleries of the Draper allow visitors close access to real-life dramas from the Greater Yellowstone region.

right: Draper exhibitions and programs focus on Yellowstone and Grand Teton National Parks and the surrounding landscapes.

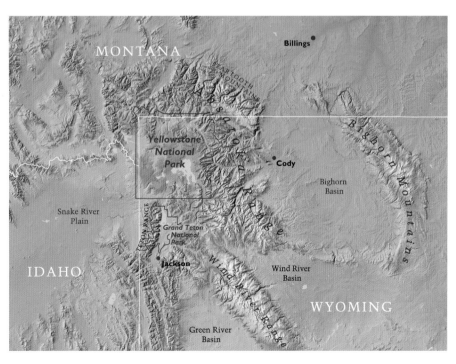

C.R. Preston

The high, craggy peaks of alpine environments in the Greater Yellowstone region are home to native Rocky Mountain bighorn sheep during summer months and non-native mountain goats year-round. Wildlife artist Carl Rungius captured a typical alpine summer scene in his painting *The Mountaineers*, which interprets this spectacular, top-of-the-world environment.

This bighorn sheep ram was confiscated from poachers by the Wyoming Game and Fish Department who provided it to the Draper for exhibition. NH.305.17

Elephanthead lousewort is one of many colorful wildflowers that adorn summer alpine environments in the Greater Yellowstone region.

left: These little tree islands, known as krummholz or "twisted wood," mark the upper limit of tree growth and the beginning of alpine tundra in the Rocky Mountains.

Yellow-bellied marmots are active through the summer in and around alpine boulder fields. They gorge themselves on grasses and other plants to fatten up for a long winter hibernation in this harsh environment.

Draper staff and interns collect sounds from each of the environments represented in our exhibitions, providing an authentic, multi-sensory experience for our visitors.

C.R. Preston

Mountain forest environments support a wide variety of plants and animals.

right: More than 300 years of history are recorded in the growth rings of this slice of an Engelmann spruce tree that burned during the Yellowstone fires of 1988. This particular tree, known as the Camp Monaco Tree, once grew at a backcountry base camp occupied by Prince Albert I of Monaco. The expedition was guided by W.F. "Buffalo Bill" Cody.

On loan from Shoshone National Forest, L.102.2002.16

Yellowstone Fires, 1988

Blue fungus stain

Declaration of Independence 1776

top: Gray wolves sometimes establish birth dens in secluded forest openings. Pups are typically born in April and remain near the den eight to ten weeks. The gray wolf was reintroduced to the Greater Yellowstone region in 1995.

left: A male blue grouse shows off for mates in a forest opening.

center: Snowshoe hares inhabit subalpine forests in the Greater Yellowstone region. This young rabbit was captured, photographed, and released in the Shoshone National Forest southwest of Cody.

right: Draper staff, interns, and volunteers conduct field expeditions to explore, document, and interpret for the public. This crew explores the high elevation forests of Carter Mountain.

Meadow Environment | *Above 6,000 feet*

Primarily found between 6,000–8,000 feet, mountain meadow/aquatic environments come in a variety of shapes and sizes, but typically include standing water and moist soils much of the growing season. Grasses, sedges, and willows usually dominate the vegetation.

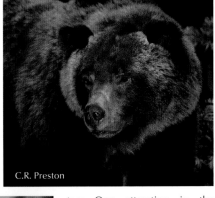

C.R. Preston

C.R. Preston

C.R. Preston

C.R. Preston

top: One attraction in the Mountain Meadow Environment is Grizzly Bear 104. During her life, she often lingered on open hillsides within sight of the roadway. This 19-year-old sow was struck and killed by a truck in the Shoshone National Forest near the east entrance to Yellowstone National Park. DRA.305.4

left: A bird in hand . . . Lincoln's sparrows are abundant during summer in shrubby meadows. This adult male was captured and released as part of the Draper's field-based educational programming.

left center: Draper science program volunteers learn to capture, identify, and release birds unharmed using special "mist" nets.

bottom left: Mountain meadows support a variety of plant species, including wildflowers like this Rocky Mountain columbine.

far left: The beaver is often referred to as a "keystone" species, because it exerts widespread influence on its surroundings. By damming streams, beavers sometimes create ponds with surrounding meadows that support a variety of plants and animals. The exhibition features a "walk-in" beaver lodge, complete with a willow thicket and moose.

C.R. Preston

Dry plains/basin environments that occupy much of the landscape of the Greater Yellowstone region are usually dominated by dramatic rock outcrops and various species of sagebrush.

Prairie dog burrows provide shelter for many animals, and prairie dogs are important prey for some predators. These two ferruginous hawks are challenging one another for a prairie dog meal. In the Draper, visitors can come eye-to-eye with these fascinating birds of prey.

top right: Free-ranging bison once roamed the plains and basins surrounding Yellowstone and Grand Teton National Parks. Draper staff lead field tours into the parks so people can see and learn about native bison firsthand.

right: The pronghorn antelope is one of the few animal species that regularly eats the bitter leaves of sagebrush. Well-adapted for wide open country, the pronghorn has keen, long-distance eyesight, and can run at speeds greater than 60 miles per hour!

lower right: Golden eagles are a continuing research focus for Draper staff, interns, and volunteers. This researcher is standing below a large golden eagle nest that may be more than thirty years old and is still used by eagles during the breeding season.

left: When moisture is available during early spring, wildflowers such as firewheel, orange globe mallow, prickly pear cactus (shown), and prairie evening prim-rose paint the landscape with color.

McCRACKEN RESEARCH LIBRARY

DEDICATED 1980

The McCracken Research Library advances the understanding, appreciation, and study of the American West and plays an integral role in preserving scholarship on the region. With book collections in western American art and history, the natural history of the Greater Yellowstone region, Plains Indian culture, and firearms history and technology, the library is a major regional research center. The library holds more than 30,000 volumes, including rare books.

In addition to its book collections, the library has more than three hundred manuscript collections related to the history, science, and art of the American West. One of the largest and most important collections is the William F. Cody Archive, which includes personal correspondence, Wild West show programs, route books, scrapbooks, pulp novels, sheet music, poetry, photographs, and ephemera. Together with the Buffalo Bill Museum collection, the archive provides an overview of Cody's life and career, as well as insight into Cody as an individual and showman.

Other manuscript collections document the lives and works of important western illustrators and artists such as James Bama, Frank Tenney Johnson, W.H.D. Koerner, and Joseph H. Sharp. The library also has a significant collection of historic photographs from such notable national and regional photographers as D.F. Barry, Charles Belden, Edward Curtis, F.J. Hiscock, L.A. Huffman, Thomas Marquis, Rev. William A. Petzoldt, Jack Richard, and F.A. Rinehart.

These collections document the rich variety of western experience, including the frontier era and the establishment of settlements and ranches. In addition they portray native peoples, both in the photographer's studio and in the natural environment, capturing intimate scenes of family life and traditional activities. Iconic views of the American cowboy as a stylish, heroic type are represented as well as a cowboy's stark lonely life on the vast western plains. The collection also includes works by many important photographers who made pilgrimages to Yellowstone National Park, seeing it as both a remarkable tourist attraction and a natural wonder.

Library materials are available to staff, visiting scholars, as well as Buffalo Bill Historical Center patrons and visitors.

above and right:
John S. Hart
The Iris: an Illuminated Souvenir for MDCCCLII
Philadelphia: Lippincott, Grambo & Co., 1851

A color printing process called chromolithography was used to illustrate nineteenth century books. This exquisite example showcases the paintings of Captain Charles Eastman, a soldier-artist who spent nine years on the frontier. The fanciful tales of Indian life illustrated here were written by the artist's wife, Mary Eastman.

Gift of the Honorable and Mrs. Wallace H. Johnson and Mr. and Mrs. John O. Housel, RB.AY.11.I6.1852

left:
From important works illuminating the "newly" discovered continent, to the novels of the early twentieth century, illustrated books provide an important resource for studying and understanding how Americans viewed the West.

clockwise from left: Buffalo Bill, *Story of the Wild West and Camp Fire Chats*, William F. Cody Special Collection, F591.C67.C.2; George Catlin, *North American Indians*, Gift of Sara Jorgensen, RB.E77.C3973; William Cullen Bryant, *Picturesque America*, New York: Appleton and Co., 1872, Gift of James H. Maroney, Jr., RB.E168.B79

This selection of material from the Yellowstone National Park Special Collection advertises the wonders of the region. Through illustrations, photographs, and pamphlets such as these, railroads, tour companies, and other commercial ventures hoped to lure visitors to the park.

above, clockwise from left: Yellowstone National Park Special Collection: *The Great or Lower Falls of the Yellowstone,* MS21.2.MC.10.1; F.J. Haynes, *Geyser Hill, Upper Basin,* P.21.83; Edward F. Colborn, *Where Gush the Geysers,* Union Pacific Railroad, F722.C64 1910; *Yellowstone National Park,* Northern Pacific Railway; Bill Chapman, *Yarns of Yellowstone,* F722.C52

below:
A hand-illustrated issue of *Yellowstone Nature Notes*

Gift of Yellowstone Research Library,
Yellowstone National Park, Wyoming, SB.481.Y4

Grace Raymond Hebard and Paul M. Paine
Map of the History and Romance of Wyoming, reprint, 1936

One of the many maps in the library collection, this map traces the exploration and settlement of Wyoming from pre-territorial days to the present.

Gift of Miss Lola Homsher, F761.H42

Gen. G.A. Custer
My Life on the Plains
New York: Sheldon and Co., 1874

The Indian Wars period, 1865–1890, was one of conflict and change in the American West. Books, maps, and photographs from and about this period form an important core collection in the McCracken Research Library.

Gift of Paul M. Fulks, Sr., RB.F594.C97

Several comprehensive collections shed light on the daily activities, artistic techniques, and business interests of western artists and illustrators. Sculptors and painters often worked from their own photographs, and these collections remain significant to research. This is a photograph of one of the numerous studies of the sculpture, *Mustangs,* in plaster cast form. The sculptor himself is visible at lower right seated in the shadow of this dramatic, monumental piece.

Alexander Phimister Proctor Collection,
Gift of Phimister and Sally Church,
Phimister Proctor Foundation, P.242.OS9.9.6.2

The spirit of the American West has long been captured in song. From cowboy songs and range ballads to songs from Buffalo Bill's Wild West show, the McCracken Research Library preserves the musical heritage of the West in both written and recorded form.

clockwise from left: Gene Williams, *Wyoming Lullaby*, Gift of Joseph Macchia, MS224.1.63; William Sweeney, *Buffalo Bill's Farewell March and Two Step*, 1911, William F. Cody Collection, MS6.1.D.OS1.4.2; Benedetto Cerato, *A l'Intrepide Colonel Cody, Grands Marche*, 1906, William F. Cody Collection, MS6.1.D.OS1.4.1; Harry Starr, *Buffalo Bill, The Wild West Show*, Peter H. Davidson Collection, MS6.6.D.OS1.1

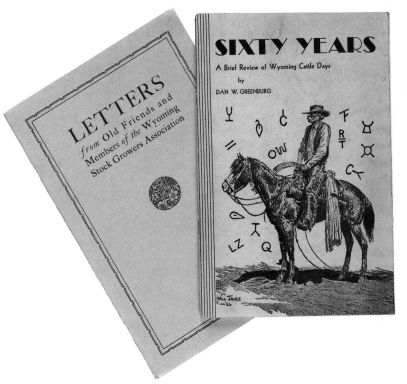

left:
These rare documents celebrate and trace the history of the cattle industry in Wyoming.

Letters from Old Friends and Members of the Wyoming Stockgrowers Association, 1923, Gift of Barron G. Collier II, RB.HD.9417.W8.L477.1923; *Sixty Years, A Brief Review of Wyoming Cattle Days*, 1932, Gift of Jack Caldwell, RB.HD.9417.W9G74.1932

The W.F. "Buffalo Bill" Cody archive is one of the largest collections of personal and business correspondence in the library. Letters from Cody to close friends reveal the man behind the showman. The stresses of maintaining a daily performance schedule for more than thirty seasons of Buffalo Bill's Wild West show, as well as a lively sense of humor, are apparent in this letter.

letter, *My Dear Geary*, July 5, 1901
Gift of Diane Fay in memory of Bertram W. Raymond, MS6.1.B.1.16.10

Dude ranching flourished as an industry in northern Wyoming and grew in importance as a tourist enterprise across the West in the early twentieth century. Brochures such as these reflect the character of individual ranches and portray the lively attractions of the western experience.

Original Buffalo Bill Museum Collection:
The Dude Rancher, Nov. 1935,
GV.198.945.D83;
Ranch Life in the Buffalo Bill Country,
1920s, GV.198.96.W8.R36.1927a;
Eaton's Ranch, 1921,
GV.198.96.W8.E28.1921

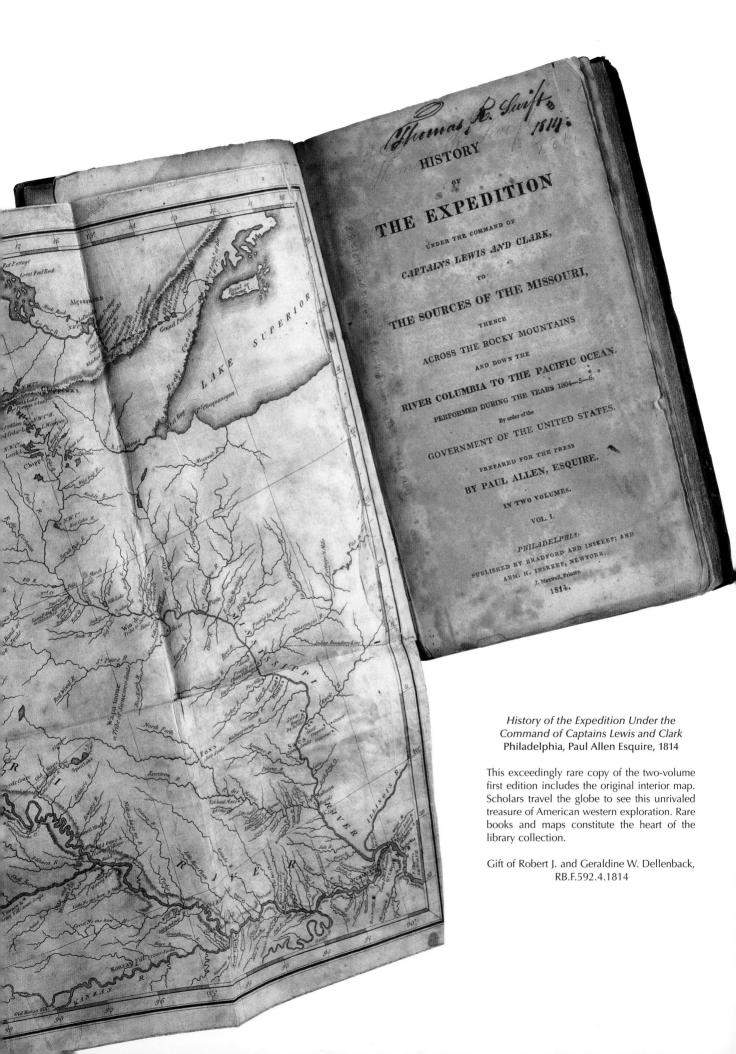

*History of the Expedition Under the
Command of Captains Lewis and Clark*
Philadelphia, Paul Allen Esquire, 1814

This exceedingly rare copy of the two-volume
first edition includes the original interior map.
Scholars travel the globe to see this unrivaled
treasure of American western exploration. Rare
books and maps constitute the heart of the
library collection.

Gift of Robert J. and Geraldine W. Dellenback,
RB.F.592.4.1814

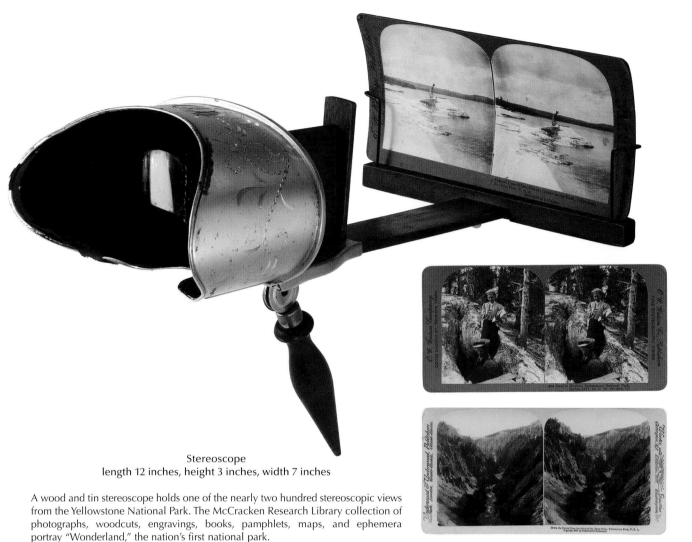

Stereoscope
length 12 inches, height 3 inches, width 7 inches

A wood and tin stereoscope holds one of the nearly two hundred stereoscopic views from the Yellowstone National Park. The McCracken Research Library collection of photographs, woodcuts, engravings, books, pamphlets, maps, and ephemera portray "Wonderland," the nation's first national park.

stereocards, top down: Yellowstone National Park Collection: *Famous Cone Where Fish are Cooked on the Hook, Yellowstone National Park,* ST.21.184; *Devil's Kitchen, Yellowstone National Park,* ST.21.98; *Down the Canyon from the Brink of the Great Falls, Yellowstone Park, U.S.A.,* ST.21.124; *In the Village of Blackfeet Indians near St. Mary's Lake, Glacier National Park, Montana,* Vincent J. Mercaldo Collection, P.71.1065

Original photographs, like those of frontier photographer L.A. Huffman, offer rare views, including the last of the free-ranging buffalo herds and portraits of native peoples. These early images are considered some of the best of their era. The McCracken Research Library houses important historic photographs of Crow, Northern Cheyenne, Blackfeet, and Lakota peoples, as well as a documentary history of Buffalo Bill's Wild West show that includes Native American cast members, star performers like Annie Oakley, and glimpses of life backstage.

left to right:
L.A. Huffman Collection, Museum purchase: gelatin silver print, *Two Bow Gun Boys,* 1895, P.100.3616; collotype, *Chief Two Moon'¡s Teepee, Lame Deer Agency,* 1896, P.100.1952; *Mrs. White Elk, Cheyenne,* P.100.1943

The Buffalo Bill Historical Center enjoys a reputation as the world's foremost Western American museum complex. It features the Buffalo Bill Museum, the Whitney Gallery of Western Art, the Plains Indian Museum, the Cody Firearms Museum, the Draper Museum of Natural History, and the McCracken Research Library. The Buffalo Bill Historical Center is located amid some of the grandest vistas of the northern Rocky Mountains in the historic town of Cody, Wyoming.

PUBLISHER:
Buffalo Bill Historical Center
720 Sheridan Avenue
Cody, Wyoming 82414
307.587.4771 • www.bbhc.org

PROJECT MANAGER:
Elizabeth Holmes

PROJECT COORDINATION:
Kimber Swenson
Tiffany Swain Olson
Susan Ahalt

EDITOR:
Dan Hinderaker
Worland, Wyoming

IMAGE RIGHTS AND REPRODUCTIONS:
Ann Marie Donoghue

DESIGNER:
Jan Woods-Krier — ProDesign
Cody, Wyoming

DIGITAL IMAGING:
Mark Schuler — ProDesign
Cody, Wyoming
Sean Campbell

PHOTOGRAPHY:
Buffalo Bill Historical Center
Staff photographers (unless noted)

AUTHORED BY:
Buffalo Bill Historical Center staff

PRINTED BY:
Shearson Print Group
411 Washington Avenue North, Suite 20
Minneapolis, Minnesota 55401

Sung In Printing, Korea

INTERNATIONAL STANDARD BOOK NUMBER
978-0-931618-64-9

This book available at:
Museum Selections ■ 800.533.3838 ■ www.bbhcstore.com